TO GET TO YOU

HOW TO IMPROVE YOUR RELATIONSHIP, OVERCOME CONFLICTS, AND ENHANCE INTIMACY

COMMUNICATION BOOK FOR COUPLES

Solomon Francis

Table of Contents

Falling in love is great. The first few months of love makes you feel like you are walking on clouds. Bird song surrounds you, the city you live in no longer boring and gray, but full of beauty and wonder. Love, at first, is fireworks, passion and romance. Walks on the beach, hand holding, gazing into each other's eyes in the restaurant. You will think your partner can do no wrong. You worship the ground they walk upon, thinking that no other human can be this perfect. The honeymoon phase, if you're lucky, can last up to two years. Then, eventually you will realize that actually no humans are perfect and so your partner is not perfect either.

The honeymoon period comes to an end. Life takes over. You realize your partner is just a human too, but a great one! But, still, they kind of can be annoying, and things might not go as smoothly as you thought they would. Annoying habits seem to take hold. Differences over priorities. In-laws create arguments. But, this does not mean your relationship is over. It just means that you are human, and you have problems and therefore you need to communicate! Conflict does not mean that you're not in love. Conflict is normal and ultimately necessary to build a long-lasting relationship. All you need to do is be able to communicate these issues in a healthy and constructive way.

Communication is important in all aspects of our lives. Humans are naturally social creatures and we use words and language daily to make solid connections with others. However, when it comes to romantic relationships, communication can be neglected, and conflict often arises from poor talking and listening skills. Good communication is a fundamental part of any healthy relationship and without it, a relationship will fail.

This book is essential in any healthy relationship. It will help you create a basic understanding of communication skills and how to apply them to your current or future relationship. Using professional techniques and tips in easy and accessible ways, it will provide you with the framework for a healthy and successful relationship. It will look at professional and psychological help that relationship counselors have created, such as Gary Chapman's *Five Love Languages*. This will help you understand love and communication in a simple and new way, and as something to work on. Love is not just about passion and lust, but companionship and respect.

For readers in a stable relationship, this book will help you strengthen your bond and provide ways to build on your successes. It will provide ways in which you can keep the love alive, avoiding boredom and conflict. For those in a relationship that is failing, this book is key to address the issues that you may be facing. It will help shine a light on the core problems that cause conflict and provide ways in which you can find resolutions and avoid future issues. This book is also important for single people to read, as it will provide crucial advice on how to make sure their next relationship is healthy and stable.

This book will approach issues that a lot of relationships face. Unfortunately, arguments about money, sex, trust and priorities are common occurrences in relationships, and all have the same root cause: lack of communication. In discussing the common arguments and problems that many couples experience, it is clear that these all can be solved with good communication. This book provides guidelines on how to approach topics in a respectful and productive way. It will also provide an outline of what a healthy relationship should be, as modern media, films and TV can skew our perceptions. Relationships require work, but they are ultimately about fun and companionship. It is important to know warning signs and red flags in your partner and to know when to walk away. Self-care is more important than any relationship.

This book will also address the importance of communication in regard to our sex lives. It is completely normal to get stuck in a sexual rut, and even if the rest of your relationship is great, it can be a difficult topic to discuss. This book will provide ways of communication in and out of the bedroom that can improve your sex life. It will approach these topics in a sex-positive way, showing that your sex life is just as important as other factors in your relationship.

This book will provide ways to keep the honeymoon phase going, suggesting that it is possible for this phase to last a lifetime! In finding new ways to reconnect with one another and enjoy your life in and outside of the relationship, you will find yourself falling in love with your partner time and time again.

CHAPTER 1
FOUNDATIONS OF A HEALTHY LOVE

Figure 1

Hollywood films depict love as earth-shattering, intense and obsessive. Many films suggest that love isn't love unless you would die for that person and that a proper relationship is when you are completely consumed by one another. It isn't just films, it's TV, the books we read and the music we listen to. But, these aren't signs of a healthy relationship. In fact, more often than not, these types of relationships are unhealthy, counter-productive and therefore ultimately doomed. This chapter will discuss what a healthy relationship looks like in regard to conflict and empathy. It will also give advice on how to spot warning signs and red flags that suggest that breaking up is the best thing to do. There is no such thing as a perfect relationship, things work differently for every couple.

However, there are certain values that underpin every healthy relationship that are the foundations for a long-lasting and enjoyable love.

CORE NEEDS

When discussing our relationships with friends and family, there is a tendency to focus on the negatives. Your partner may do something irritating that you don't like, or fail to do the chores one day. These little things can build up, and it is important to address these things. However, it is also important to focus on the positives in your relationship you may overlook. Here, take a step back and look at your relationship as if you were an outsider. Are there good signs that your relationship is healthy? This section will examine the core needs of a healthy relationship and give advice on how they may be cultivated. For those that are single, knowing factors that make a healthy relationship is extremely important when going out into the dating world. At the core of a relationship, the most important thing is that it brings more happiness than stress for the people involved.

EMPATHY

Empathy is a skill that everyone has access to. However, many of us might find it difficult to use it in the correct way. It is important to have empathy in a relationship, and even more important to have the right type. To understand it more, psychologists have broken down empathy into three categories; cognitive, emotional and compassionate. Cognitive empathy is the one we use most of the time. It is where we can understand a person is feeling a certain way but we don't share their emotions. We can gain insight into our partner's moods by noticing body language and communicating with them. When it comes to caring for your partner, cognitive empathy runs the risk of being emotionally removed from the situation. You are not fully putting yourself in your partner's shoes and this can cause friction and arguments in the relationship. It is important to fully understand and sympathize with your partner in order to create an open and balanced relationship. Emotional empathy is when you feel what the other person is feeling; for example, if your partner is anxious, you may feel anxious too. This response is hard wired in our brains, with lots of animals, including humans, having been observed to have "mirror neurons". These mirror neurons fire both when the animal is doing a certain action or when the animal is perceiving another doing the same action. Having this intense type of empathy can sometimes cause issues in relationships and it is important to distinguish between your emotions and your partner's emotions. If we become too emotionally empathic with our partner, we run the risk of getting stuck in negative thought cycles as neither individual has the power to help the other out.

Compassionate empathy is a mix of both cognitive and emotional empathy and is important in a healthy relationship. When we have compassionate empathy, we understand our partner is feeling in such a way and have emotions similar to them and this pushes us to act. It is using emotional intelligence to help our loved ones and allows us to find solutions to situations we find ourselves in.

If you are in a relationship, think about what type of empathy you most relate to. Are you too removed from your partner's emotions or too involved? Both can be problematic in regard to a healthy relationship. In order to develop compassionate empathy, we must communicate with our partners and keep note of how we are feeling ourselves.

Imagine your partner has just had a loss in their family. In an unhealthy relationship, empathy may be either too emotional or too cognitive. For example, if you feel intense grief and act as upset and heartbroken as your partner, this empathy is too emotional. This is unfair to your partner and does not help them one bit. They are in need of your support right now. If you feel too removed from the situation and tell your partner you understand they are upset and you are sorry, this may be too cognitive a response and may push your partner away during their difficult time.

What would the correct response be in regard to empathy? The best for both your relationship and your partner is to cultivate a compassionate empathetic response. Understand your partner's grief, feel some of the sadness too, but look at ways you can help them. Allow yourself to communicate with each other about both your feelings and how your actions may improve the situation.

SUPPORT

A relationship needs to be an environment where both participants feel supported and comfortable. It is important that both you and your partner feel mutually benefited and helped during the good times and the bad times that either of you may face.

A supportive relationship means that you respect each other's individuality. You are a person with your own needs and goals. Your partner is too, and in order to create a safe and healthy space for each other, you need to fully support the ambitions, life plans and priorities of the other. This can be hard, especially when you feel you may not fully understand their choices in life. Here, communication and honesty is key. You should be able to give your partner advice, but you should not expect them to always take it. In discussing their choices and goals, you are being supportive. Respect their decisions, remember that they are a separate person from you. Believe in them but also do not be afraid to call them out for things you do not agree with. A relationship should be built on equality and respect, and thus can survive and remain healthy throughout disagreements if you are open and honest with each other.

In creating a supportive relationship, it may sometimes feel one sided. If your partner is going through a tough time, or keeps causing issues with work or family, this may give rise to friction and conflict in your relationship. Here, it is important to remember that you are your own individual person and self-care is important. Also try to empathize with your partner's mindset. What would you need in their situation to feel supported? Can you discuss how their actions or problems are making you feel? When supporting a partner through illness or trauma, it is important to take care of yourself and how you feel. Know that your partner would do the same thing to support you.

TRUST

Paranoia and jealousy can cause intense conflict in a relationship and often ultimately destroys them. This means that trust is one of the most important core needs that underpin healthy love. However, building trust can be hard. Many of us are often affected by previous relationships, where a previous partner may have cheated or been hurtful towards us. Here, it is important to know that your current partner is not your ex. This sounds like an obvious statement, but in regard to trust, it is often forgotten. Whatever has happened to you will not automatically happen again.

How much trust is in your relationship at the moment? Do you both have respect for each other's privacy?

If trust is an issue, you need to say exactly what you mean when discussing these problems. Ask yourself these questions:

- Do you have any proof that you should not trust your partner?
- Is it realistic that there may be things to distrust about your partner?
- Is it helpful to distrust your partner?

When facing your trust issues with these three questions, you will probably come to the conclusion that there is no reason to be distrustful. If certain things come up from these questions, you must discuss them with your partner. If you find that there is no reason to be distrustful, you can build on your healthy trust and support in your relationship.

When building trust, you need to say what you mean to your partner. It is important to be truthful and therefore allow them to be truthful to you. Give yourself the chance to be vulnerable to your partner, too, and take a leap of faith in the relationship. Building trust means opening up, and this runs the risk of being hurt, but if you do not take the risk you will not reap the benefits of a healthy and supportive relationship.

If you have been lied to or cheated on, it may take you a long time to get over this with a new partner. Here, communication is the most important thing. Allow yourself to express your worries to your new partner. If you are rebuilding a relationship after an infidelity, time helps to heal these issues. You will not just trust your partner again straight away. Listen to each other and communicate your feelings. Try to understand why the infidelity happened. If you are serious about overcoming this within your relationship, you need to cast your doubts aside and open yourself up to trusting your partner again. Remain in the present, and do not keep returning past feelings and mistakes. Truly listen to your partner and their needs and allow them to listen to yours.

It is important to know that not all relationships can be worked on, and sometimes it is better for both involved to walk away. Ultimately, your mental and physical wellbeing is more important than any relationship.

CONFLICT

How often do you and your partner fight? Conflict and arguments are a normal part of a relationship and there is a big difference between healthy and unhealthy conflict. When you do not argue with your partner, there is a risk of passivity and emotions being ignored. We are all individuals with different needs and views and it is a part of life to disagree with your partner. However, it is how couples face these issues that distinguishes between healthy and unhealthy conflict. In approaching conflict in a healthy way, it is important to stay focused on the problem at hand. If the argument is about chores, try to find solutions and stay on the topic of chores. Figure out how to solve the issue. Do not allow this to become a free for all on things that your partner does that upsets you or has upset you. Do not bring up past issues.

It is important to learn the difference between solvable and perpetual issues. Perpetual issues are about you as a person, such as personality traits. You or your partner cannot change these. Therefore, it is unhealthy to argue about these issues. Turn your attention to solvable issues. If it is about the chores, you can figure it out. When you concentrate on solving issues that are solvable, you and your partner will feel close and more aware of each other. This means that arguments can ultimately lead to growth in the relationship. In discussing and hashing out your issues in a respectful and productive way, you and your partner can overcome difficulty and let the problem be a thing of the past.

When you are in a relationship, you need to communicate and argue fairly. If arguments become abusive, with personal attacks and raised voices, it is time to leave the relationship. If arguments become physical, with pushing or hitting, it is time to leave the relationship.

Figure 2

It may sound odd, but not having any verbal arguments in a relationship may be a warning sign. If you and your partner cannot communicate with each other when things are wrong, it can create a whole load of underlying resentment and suffering. You are not a mind reader, and neither is your partner, so it is unhealthy to think you know what is going on in the other person's head.

Furthermore, shutting your partner out is a sign of unhealthy conflict. If you or your partner withdraw for days at a time, this is a sign of toxic arguing. In not being verbal about the issues you are facing, you are not getting rid of the problem, rather just letting it fester. It will keep coming up again and again. If you and your partner are unable to communicate your feelings and issues with one another, then you cannot progress as a couple. It is unfair to both of you and is a sign of an unhealthy relationship. If one of you is constantly shutting the other out, you cannot fully enjoy your relationship.

TOXIC RELATIONSHIPS

Toxic relationships cannot be worked on. It affects your happiness, your self-esteem and your own personal growth. Therefore, it is necessary to leave the relationship. A healthy relationship can quickly turn toxic if needs aren't met and communication has stalled. However, a lot of people are unaware of the signs of toxic relationships.

Look at your relationship and ask yourself, is it affecting your life negatively? Does it affect your relationship with your friends and family? How about work and your career? And, most importantly, are you happy?

If the relationship feels mostly bad, it is toxic and you need to leave. If you are constantly arguing and finding no resolution, this is a red flag for a toxic relationship. Does it have any of the core needs discussed earlier in the chapter? Is there trust? Empathy? Support?

Remember, if there is more sadness and pain than fun in the relationship, it is not worth it. Self care and safety is more important than any relationship. A successful relationship is built on a shared enjoyment for life and respect for one another. Toxic relationships means that this is lacking. More often than not, when a relationship is toxic it cannot be fixed. Respect is necessary from both individuals to make a relationship work and a toxic relationship is defined by a lack of respect. Remember to love yourself just as much and maybe even more than your partner.

SIGNS OF ABUSE

It is important to know that strong and independent people can fall into abusive relationships. There is no one type of victim when it comes to abuse, and abuse comes in all different forms. It is also possible to be abused and not even know it.

These are some signs of emotional and mental abuse that you may not know about or recognize in your relationships or the relationships of your friends and family.

Constant put downs.

- Humiliating or embarrassing you in front of others.
- Controlling money.
- Ignoring or excluding you.
- Extreme moodiness.
- Withdrawal of affection.
- Isolating you from friends and family.
- Having a lack of privacy.

If you are recognizing any of this behavior in your relationship, it is important to break off the relationship as these are things that cannot be fixed. Furthermore, if you feel scared of your partner and in need of support, there are charities and helplines available to you.

If there is any physical violence in your relationship you must walk away and if you feel comfortable, contact the police. Domestic violence is a crime. There is no helping a relationship that includes violence and it becomes unsafe and damaging for both parties involved. It is important to know that if someone is violent to you, they will most likely do it again. Apologies and romantic gestures mean nothing when coming from a violent person.

JEALOUSY

Jealousy is normal. When it comes to our partners, we mostly do not want to see them flirting or getting physically close with another. However, too much jealousy can lead to unhealthy relationship behaviors and it is important to recognize when our jealousy is taking over.

In relationships, we are protective over our partners, however, sometimes we let our jealousy grow into paranoia or obsession. This is dangerous as it can completely ruin a relationship.

Unhealthy jealousy is when you or your partner constantly wants to know where the other person is. With jealousy comes the worry that the other person is cheating, and therefore we think that knowing where they are solves this worry. However, this just pushes the person away and creates a destructive and unhealthy balance in the relationship.

Other signs of unhealthy jealousy include lack of privacy and monitoring of social media or cellphone. It is important in a relationship to have privacy and be able to be trusted with that. If there is no trust, there is no hope for the relationship.

If warning signs of jealousy appear in a relationship, it is necessary to tackle them head on. Think about your own self-esteem and why you might be feeling jealousy or fear of cheating. If it is your partner displaying unhealthy jealousy behavior, try and have an open discussion about the reasons for this. When confronted as soon as the warning signs appear, these unhealthy relationship behaviors can be altered and communication can be worked on.

CHAPTER 2
LOVE LANGUAGES

The psychologist and marriage counselor Gary Chapman developed the idea that there are five love languages. These are how we show our love to our partner, and Chapman suggests that problems within marriage and relationships occur when we are not using the correct love language. People do not express and receive love in the same way. There is not a correct, one size fits all way to show and receive love, and using the idea of love languages means that we can clearly tell our partner how we wish to receive love. In identifying with one or more of the love languages we are able to communicate with our partner what we want in our relationship and how we want to be loved. Knowing your love language also impacts on how you give love to your partner. Love languages give you emotional awareness of giving and receiving love.

In order to discover your love language, you need to observe how you show love to others. This is often an indicator of how you wish to be loved yourself. Also ask yourself what it is that you find yourself asking for most from your partner. If you tend to ask them to do chores around the house, it suggests that your love language is acts of service. If you often find yourself asking your partner for hugs, then your love language is most likely physical touch. This chapter will go through all five love languages and suggest ways to implement them in your relationship.

If after this chapter you still cannot work out what love language is yours, find a quiz on the internet. There are loads of resources out there that will help you discover your love language. Go into this with an open mind. You may be surprised at what your love language actually is!

WORDS OF AFFIRMATION

According to Chapman, many couples underestimate the power of words in a relationship, yet verbal encouragement and compliments are the main love language. Words are a powerful tool in strengthening a relationship and showing your partner you love them. This may be your love language if you sometimes think that you don't hear "I love you" from your partner enough. This may be your love language if you feel a buzz from compliments that you receive from your partner.

GIVING THIS TYPE OF LOVE

If your partner identifies with the words of affirmation love language, there are many ways you can use this to show your love. Verbal compliments are always welcome. If your partner is wearing a new dress, tell them that they look great in that new dress. Tell them they are kind and caring. Remind them that you love them.

Encouraging words are also important in creating a supportive and empathic relationship. Think of what your partner may be insecure about. Perhaps there is a promotion up for grabs at your partner's place of work. They might be lacking courage and confidence to apply. But, using words of encouragement gives your partner the support they will need to go for the promotion. Remind them that they are smart and hardworking. This will give them confidence and further strengthen your relationship. Supporting one another is a core need of a relationship.

Be aware of how you talk to your partner, especially if their love language is words of affirmation, the way these words are said is just as important as the words themselves. Make sure you are kind and gentle with your words, knowing their power in your relationship.

RECEIVING THIS TYPE OF LOVE

If this is your love language, open up the conversation about it with your significant other. Do not outright ask for compliments, and this will run the risk of feeling like the love is insincere. Rather, bring up the topic of love languages to your partner and suggest ways of implementing them in your relationship. Tell your partner that you need words of encouragement and support.

Don't forget to tell your partner you love them. This will prompt them to say it back. This reassurance of love can be necessary for you if your love language is words of affirmation. In repeating this statement every day, you are reminding each other of your love, and this will give you both confidence and strengthen your relationship.

QUALITY TIME

This love language means giving your partner your undivided attention. It is more than just being in each other's company while you live your life. Rather, it is about setting out time to give to your partner. If you or your partner complains that in the relationship you don't do things as a couple, then this might be your love language.

GIVING THIS TYPE OF LOVE

If this is your partner's love language, it is important to cultivate a feeling of togetherness. To do this, focus your attention on your partner and your partner alone. Put your phone on silent, turn the TV off and just talk. This feeling of togetherness can also be found in joint activities. Going out for a walk with your significant other, or taking a class together are fun ways to engage in quality time together.

Quality time also means quality conversations. This means to engage your partner in sympathetic dialogue, sharing thoughts and feelings with each other. Listen to your partner's pains, wishes and needs. Remember to put time aside each day to create this quality conversational time. Observe your partner's body language, maintain eye contact and do not interrupt them when they are talking. Take turns to talk, and really listen to what each other is saying. Afterward, you will both feel respected and comfortable in your relationship.

RECEIVING THIS TYPE OF LOVE

If this is your type of love language, try and set a date night for you and your partner at least once a month. Go for dinner or go play mini golf or bowling. This will give you the important quality time that you are seeking in your relationship. This will also be pleasant for your partner, whose love language might be different, as doing things you enjoy together as a couple will bring you closer together. Let your partner know that you really appreciate the time you spend together doing activities.

A great way to spend quality time together is to try something new! This also avoids your relationship getting stuck in a routine. Be willing to try new activities. Have you ever been kayaking before? No? Why don't you try it with your partner? Even if you both hate it, it will be a memory to cherish, and a reason to spend time with each other.

RECEIVING GIFTS

This might be your love language if you are one of those people who, when out shopping, buys loved ones trinkets and small gifts. You do this because when you see these gifts, you are reminded of certain friends or family members. This is not a love language of the greedy or materialistic, as gifts are about being thoughtful of your partner when you are apart. It can be as simple picking up a rock on the beach for your loved one. It is not what the gift is, but rather what it symbolizes. It symbolizes that a person is on your mind even when not together.

GIVING THIS TYPE OF LOVE

If this is your partner's love language, don't get overwhelmed! You don't need to buy them expensive jewelry or flash outfits. For this type of love language, the gift itself does not matter. The cost of it does not matter. Gifts can be bought, but they also can be found or made. When coming home from work, stop and pick flowers from the side of the road for your partner. When picking up your weekly groceries, grab your partner's favorite chocolate bar. These are tokens of your love.

Figure 3

Handmade gifts are probably the most sacred for a person whose love language is receiving gifts. It doesn't even matter if you are not crafty! The quality of the gift is not important. Making a card is a great gift for your partner. Cut a love heart out and write your names in. Sprinkle glitter on it! This will be cherished by your loved one. You could even enroll in craft classes, such as wood carving or ceramics. In doing this, your partner will be extremely touched by your willingness to take on their love language.

RECEIVING THIS TYPE OF LOVE

If your love language is receiving gifts, you may feel like this is a difficult topic to approach with your partner. If you find it hard to tell them your wants, perhaps take it upon yourself to open up this love language within your relationship. Making sure the gifts are free help, and you can use nature to guide you in your gifting. Go out in nature, and if you see something that reminds you of them, give it to your partner, tell them you saw it and thought of them. They will be touched and next time they are out in nature they will think of the gift and bring something back for you!

Be aware of the gift of self that your partner gives you, and be open to them about your appreciation of this gift. Tell them that their presence is the best gift you can receive.

ACTS OF SERVICE

If you find yourself annoyed at the fact your partner has not washed the dishes or mowed the lawn, then this might be your love language. Acts of service is about doing things that you know your partner would like you to do. For people whose love language is acts of service, words and gifts do not always show love. Actions speak louder than words, and doing things to support your partner is the most important way of showing love.

GIVING THIS TYPE OF LOVE

If this is your partner's love language, try and do things that will make their life flow more smoothly and be a little easier. Cooking a meal or doing DIYs around the house are perfect ways to show your partner your love. If your partner is stressed with work and has a list of errands to run, take that list from them and complete some. This eases the load off their plate and also shows them you love them. Also don't forget to outright ask your significant other what it is that they want you to do! Maybe get them to write a list for you? If you have a free afternoon, ask them if they need anything done around the house or if they have any errands to run.

Perhaps this is one of the easiest love languages to learn. It is a reminder that love is about equality and helping one another to enjoy life. It creates a healthy and solid relationship that focuses on real things that can help the person you love.

RECEIVING THIS TYPE OF LOVE

Do not demand things from your partner, rather request them. Tell your partner, "I would really appreciate it if you mowed the lawn today." Make sure that they are aware you feel loved with actions and help. Be aware of tone when you are talking to your partner about acts of service. Avoid nagging, and be vocal about how much you appreciate it when they do things. Compliment them and remind them of your love when asking them to do acts of service. This creates a harmonious balance in your relationship.

Figure 4

PHYSICAL TOUCH

This love language focuses on the importance of physical touch in a relationship and how touching can communicate love. Think of what you ask from your partner in day to day life. Do you find yourself asking them for a hug, or for a back rub? Are requests for physical contact the majority of what you ask from them? If so, this may be your love language. This love language is not just about sex, but rather the feeling of connection that physical touch gives. For people with this love language, merely putting your hand on their leg when sat watching TV is enough to communicate love.

GIVING THIS TYPE OF LOVE

When giving this type of love, remember boundaries and do not do anything that would make you or your partner uncomfortable. It is good to be aware that when this is someone's love language, it is about much more than sex and little touches are just as, and perhaps even more, important as sexual intercourse or foreplay. Little touches are reminders to your partner that you are present and you love them. Little touches include a hand on a shoulder in the grocery store, or a hand on the waist when walking past them in the kitchen. These little touches symbolize love for your partner and provides you with a deeper connection.

Physical contact, such as hugging, is what we go to when someone is in a crisis or if someone is upset. It is just as important as words when supporting someone and is a reminder that you are there for them. If this is your partner's love language and they are crying, hold them.

This will mean the world to them. Remember that the body is for touching and we have receptors all over our bodies ready to feel things, be it sexual or non-sexual. These receptors mean that touching anywhere can be signs of love to our partner. Also, listen to your partner and ask them where they like to be touched. Let them be a guide for you. Some touches might show love more than others, and therefore to be aware of these means that you are able to show love more.

RECEIVING THIS TYPE OF LOVE

Again, when receiving this love, it is necessary to be aware of boundaries. Perhaps the best way to approach this love language is through discussion with your significant other about each other's wants and needs. Be vocal about the importance of physical touch, both sexual and non-sexual. Discuss with your partner how hugs can be beneficial for your health and wellbeing. Did you know that scientific studies have shown that hugs release oxytocin in the brain (Waring, 2006)? This is a hormone that decreases stress and promotes relaxation.

Talk to your partner about this. Reach out your hand to theirs. Both of you will benefit from loving touches.

Arguments and conflict are an important part of a healthy relationship. In order to create a strong and stable relationship, communication is key, even if certain conversations can be difficult and upsetting to have. No relationship will ever be perfect, but creating an open and transparent space to have healthy discussions will only benefit both partners. This chapter will look at common conflicts that arise in a relationship and provide advice on healthy ways to deal with them. It will also look at deal-breaker conflicts and red-flag problems so we are aware of issues that make or break a relationship.

HEALTHY CONFLICTS

When conflict and issues arise in a relationship, how we deal with them determines if the relationship grows stronger or weaker. Arguments do not always have to be emotionally draining and upsetting, rather ways to figure out how to build on the relationship you have.

Remember, it is more healthy to have discussions and conflicts than to avoid and ignore issues. Communication and understanding are important in building a strong relationship. Imagine your relationship as a brick wall. Every moment you share together and experience you have cement another brick in the wall. Over time this wall will become stronger, with more bricks supporting it. But, sometimes bricks might crumble away or have cracks in. We might choose to ignore the cracks and crumbles of the bricks on lower levels of the wall, but doing this only creates strain for the rest of the wall. Soon, more bricks will weaken and crumble. Instead of ignoring the cracks, take time to give them what they need. Fill the cracks in, take care of every foundation in your relationship. Then soon, the wall will become a house. A life and a home that you are able to share and enjoy together.

LITTLE THINGS

The longer that you are with someone, the more things pop up that annoy you. Perhaps before you moved in with your soulmate, you didn't think that they could possibly do anything wrong. When you are in love with someone, you normally begin with worshiping the ground they walk on. Then, after a few months or maybe a year of dating or cohabitation, little things that they do start to bug you. Does your partner leave used teabags in the sink? Do they sometimes forget to tell you they are going for a drink after work with their friends, leaving you home to eat the meal you cooked alone? These little things, when not mentioned and discussed, can be detrimental to a healthy relationship. Remember the metaphor of the wall. One brick might have a crack. It might be a small crack, but these cracks can grow. They can also cause cracks and damage to other bricks, weakening the whole structure of the wall.

This means that these small issues can cause the whole relationship to collapse.

Figure 5

Let's look at these small issues that arise and figure out ways to approach them in a healthy and communicative style. Let's look at the example of chores. Imagine a couple has just moved in together. Meg and Joshua have been dating for a few years and have finally made the plunge and Meg has moved her things into Joshua's apartment. He starts to notice things that he did not notice before when he had been visiting her home. Perhaps Meg leaves the dishes unwashed for days, piling up at the side. Perhaps she leaves dirty mugs around the apartment, not washing them until they have run out of clean ones. Joshua might at first take it upon himself to clean up after her, after she has made her breakfast and gone to work, collecting mugs from various surfaces around their home. But, after a few weeks he decides to stop doing this, to see if she starts washing her mugs and breakfast utensils. She doesn't. She might get around to cleaning up at some point but doesn't see it as an important task. For

Joshua, he prefers it when they do the dishes after their use. He doesn't like seeing them around the apartment.

Because Joshua has not mentioned this problem to Meg, resentment and annoyance is building. There is a crack in their relationship. But Meg does not understand why Joshua seems distant and moody. She has no idea what she is doing wrong.

So, how should Joshua approach this issue in a healthy way? Firstly, it is important to be direct and say exactly what he is thinking. He should also make requests instead of complaining. Instead of saying, "I hate it when you leave your dirty mugs around the house," he should say, "It would be great if you tried to clean up your mugs after their use. I just prefer it when the dishes are washed after we have used them."

He should also try and see things from Meg's perspective. Maybe Meg has just not realized that the dishes need washing, or maybe she is too busy to do them. Also, they should attempt to find some middle ground. Perhaps begin the conversation with them discussing the reasons they love living together. This allows them to take a step back and look at the bigger picture. This helps them remember that they love each other and why they decided to move in together in the first place.

If you have small conflicts in your relationship, can what we have learnt about Meg and Joshua help? Can you apply these techniques to your own relationship and learn how to deal with these conflicts in a healthy and supportive way?

In tackling these little things that create conflict in your relationship, you should also be aware of not picking on your partner and ask yourself if the problem is really a problem at all. When finding yourself being annoyed at your partner, ask yourself, "Will I be annoyed about this next week?" If not, it probably isn't worth fighting about. Maybe Meg starts to wash her dishes, but still sometimes leaves the odd mug on the bedside table for a few days. Joshua might have a twinge of annoyance when he sees the mug, but then tells himself that actually, the mug doesn't matter. What matters is his love for Meg and their relationship and the fun they are having together. He might also check in with his own issues when he finds himself being annoyed at a left mug. Sometimes we use our partner as a scapegoat for our own feelings. This is because we are around them constantly, and they are always there to listen. If Joshua has had a hard day at work, it is not Meg's mug that is causing him frustration.

When these little things occur and you find yourself wanting to have an argument with your partner, check in with your own feelings and attitudes toward your day. Take some time out and time for yourself if needed.

BIG THINGS

Unfortunately, not all conflicts are about chores or plans for a Friday night. Sometimes they are about bigger issues and really challenge a couple. When you are in a partnership, your lives are intertwined and you share so much together. Even if you are madly in love with each other, conflict about money or sex or careers can create a harmful environment when not approached in a healthy way.

In approaching a big topic that threatens your entire relationship, you must first acknowledge that it is not about you fighting your partner, it is about you both fighting against the problem. You are a team, and you support and depend on each other.

Figure 6

When approaching the big things that cause conflict in a relationship, it is useful for both people to write down what they feel and wish to say to each other. Create a list, and focus on how *you* feel, not how *they* make you feel. Sometimes these two things can be conflated and confused, and so altering the dialogue away from blame and toward conversations regarding feelings can be extremely useful. Instead of writing down "I hate it when you stay late at work, you care more about work than you do about me," say, "When you stay late at work, I feel upset and unimportant."

Now, when you both have the lists, sit down and be direct. Take turns listening to one another, and do not interrupt. A helpful idea might be to use an object such as a teddy bear or an apple. Whoever is holding this object is the one that can talk. You may feel silly at first, but this means that you can both have your say without disrespecting and interrupting one another.

Remember to really listen to your partner. Try and create breaks of silence in the discussion to think about what has been said, and to construct a respectful reply. It is fine to pause the discussion for longer than just a few seconds. If voices start to rise or interruptions happen, take an hour or even a day to cool down. Have a cup of tea, put on a comedy show, and then when you feel calmer, pick up from where you have left off. Try your best to see things from their perspective and you can only do this by fully listening and understanding their complaints and grievances. Remember to ask questions that will help you understand their side of the conflict. But do so in a respectful way. Do not say, "That does not make sense, your point is stupid," say, "I do not understand the point you are trying to make. Please can you try and explain it more." Remember not to get defensive. Take breaks if needed.

This is hard work and a slow process, but ultimately beneficial to you as a couple and you both as individuals. Remember, no couple is perfect and without conflict. It is how you deal with the conflict that strengthens or breaks a relationship. During the process of sorting out this conflict in a healthy and productive way, remember the good things in the relationship and why it is necessary to sort out the issue. There are reasons why you love each other. You make each other laugh, you enjoy so much of life together. This is part of the reason why conflict hurts so much. Your love is strong, but it will only get stronger.

UNHEALTHY CONFLICTS

Whether you are in a relationship or not, it is good to know when conflicts become unhealthy and when it is best for both of you to simply walk away. Too often couples begin to lose their individuality and own personal strengths in order to fight a losing battle. This is detrimental to health, wellbeing and most importantly time. Our time is the most precious thing we have, and so we need to be aware when we are wasting it for a dead-end relationship.

DEAL-BREAKERS

Certain things are too big for a relationship to overcome and everyone should be aware of these deal-breaker conflicts. Certain things should not be up for negotiation as they are core parts of us as humans. Other deal-breaker conflicts may seem like small issues but keep being brought up in arguments, even if the argument started because of something else. Perhaps they are a topic that you as a couple keep coming back to.

In order for a healthy relationship to blossom and be fulfilling for both individuals, both need to be aware of recurring conflict, because this might be a deal-breaker conflict. Does it ever feel like the movie *Groundhog Day*? The same conversation happening over and over again? No resolution in sight? Perhaps you have tried to talk about it peacefully and healthily, but ultimately there is no difference. The problem is still there. Maybe your partner is unwilling and unhelpful with sorting the problem out, and therefore there is more arguing than loving in the relationship. Communication is the most important thing in a relationship, and if this is gone and cannot be worked on, there is no use pursuing your future together.

Ask yourself, do you feel good about this relationship? Or are unresolved conflicts taking a toll on your wellbeing? Consider if the conflicts are resolvable or not and if both parties are willing to try and resolve them.

There are certain things that are deal-breakers, that may not cause that much conflict now, but will always be present in the relationship. These are core values and goals, and these are things that you cannot change. You may have different political or religious views, and at first you may not think that they are that much of an issue. Imagine a couple, James and David, who started dating in the summer and spend a few months going out for meals and walks, drinking cocktails and enjoying their lives. They are attracted to each other, and the sex is great, but James' political views lean left and David's lean more to the right. At first, they do not think this is a problem, they tell their friends that they just do not talk about it, but this in itself is not healthy. They are avoiding an aspect of their new partner because they don't like it.

This will never go away, no matter how hard both James and David try and ignore it. It is an indication that the relationship will not work as they are not even willing to discuss it with each other.

These core values matter when building a relationship up to last a lifetime. In regard to goals, it is important that both of you are on the same page. Again, communication is key. If you are wanting a person to share your life with, it needs to be a person who wants the same life. For example, if one person in the relationship wants kids and the other doesn't, there is no hope for the future as one will always feel resentment. You should not have to sacrifice your goals and dreams for another person. This is not what love is.

RED FLAG CONFLICT

It is first necessary to remember that relationships should be more fun than hassle. This is really what life and love comes down to. If you are arguing every day, and if you cannot remember the last time you laughed together, this is a red flag and needs to be addressed. This does not mean that relationships can't be hard. They are hard and they need work. Arguments happen. But your own personal happiness and identity is ultimately more important. If you feel like you are losing yourself, lose your partner instead. Life is too short to not be happy and to not be yourself.

As discussed, conflict is normal and healthy. Relationships need it to progress and grow stronger, and there are ways to do it that help both parties. But, if you are in a relationship or still looking for a partner, you need to be aware of red flags in conflict.

Red flags in conflict can involve control. If, when arguing, your partner seems to have the goal of control over you, then this is a problem. This can be about work, friends or family commitments. If you do not feel like you can make your own decisions without rebuttal, then the relationship is not healthy.

If conflict and arguments make you feel fear, then this is a red-flag. If you are fearful for your own safety or the safety of your partner, then it is necessary to seek help and cut the relationship off. Fear suggests that there is no trust and a significant level of uncertainty in the relationship. This is not healthy. If there is ever physical or emotional violence in conflict, then you need to leave the relationship. Name-calling and personal jibes are never acceptable and show an underlying disrespect for the victim.

In being aware of these red flags in conflict, you are able to know when it is necessary to walk away from the relationship. Sometimes, relationships cannot be worked on. This is fine. What is important is your own safety and happiness.

CHAPTER 4
CONVERSATIONS TO AND NOT TO HAVE

In creating a healthy relationship, at its core is the ability to communicate. The ability to communicate means knowing what conversations to have and what to not. It is knowing what is important in building your relationship and also what is not important. A healthy relationship means creating a space of openness and clarity, giving both individuals the opportunity to discuss and approach topics that they wish to. It is also being able to recognize what conversations might be detrimental to the relationship. In creating a successful and healthy relationship, it is necessary to know how to keep your negative thoughts away from overwhelming your positive ones.

This chapter will examine the conversations that are necessary to have in a relationship, and give examples of ones that are detrimental to both parties involved.

CONSTRUCTIVE CONVERSATIONS

There are different types of relationship-strengthening conversations and being aware of these can have a positive impact on your relationship. Creating an open and honest dialogue can lead to a high level of emotional connection which strengthens and solidifies a relationship. Certain discussions are extremely productive in creating a long lasting relationship.

CHECKING IN CONVERSATIONS

When was the last time you and your partner did a relationship check up? Have you ever? In order to create a long lasting and positive relationship, it is important to have these conversations. Try to have these every week or so and sit down with your partner and ask each other a number of questions that allow discussion to open up and problems that might be underlying be approached. Create a relaxing environment and make sure you both have time to have this discussion.

The first question to ask each other is, "How do you feel in this relationship?" This allows both parties to say honestly what they are feeling. Perhaps there is a feeling of resentment because your partner forgot to take the garbage out, or stayed out with friends too late. Perhaps you are feeling good in the relationship and have feelings of excitement. This is time to share these feelings with your partner and work on the strong relationship you have built with them.

The second question to ask them is, "How can we make this relationship stronger?" This question is very positive and healthy and focuses on the ways in which you can work on your achievements. Look at ways in which you can strengthen your relationship. Maybe it is more date nights or quality time together.

The third question to ask is, "Am I getting your love language right?" Recall the chapter about love languages and discuss this with your partner. If your love languages are different to each other, it is important to be aware of this and try and work around it. Perhaps make a list of the things that you could do to be more aware of your partner's love language and ways to fulfill them.

Figure 7

In making sure you are having "checking in conversations" at least once a month, you are creating a strong and stable relationship and allowing for progress and development both personally and as a couple.

SUPPORTIVE CONVERSATIONS

Another type of conversations that are often overlooked when relationships develop, are ones that are solely about supporting one another. In maintaining a strong relationship it is vital to continue to be vocal about support and to remind your significant other regularly that the support is there and will be for the foreseeable future. Sometimes in a relationship, we assume our partner knows that we support and care for them. However, this assumption can create conflict in the partnership, as one individual might not feel as supported as they once were. In reminding your partner you support them, they will not have worries and negative thoughts that question your support.

Knowing your partner will be there for you if you need them makes your relationship secure. This may have already been demonstrated, and you might feel comfortable in this, but ongoing support and being vocal about the support is necessary to build a healthy relationship.

There are different ways to remind your partner that you support them. Being there physically helps confirm and strengthen your attachment to each other. Physical support such as hand holding and hugs are simple ways to show support without words.

Build on physical support with supportive conversations. These can be as simple as listening and nodding to your partner's discussion and complaints about the day. Imagine John's wife Suzie has come home after a stressful day at work. Her boss has been rude and abrupt to her. Suzie sits down on the sofa with John and starts complaining about her boss. John tells her that maybe her boss is stressed and perhaps didn't mean it.

John is trying his best, wanting to let Suzie know that it isn't her fault that her boss was angry at her. However, this is not supportive to Suzie. All she needs is John to listen and nod, and say that he understands how frustrating the situation is. This shows Suzie that John is there to listen to her and support her. John can also reiterate that he supports her and always will. Just saying this statement is great as it helps

Suzie know that she is not alone in the world, and has John there to support her emotionally.

APPRECIATION CONVERSATIONS

Sometimes we forget to give appreciation to our partners. This is nothing to do with malice, you probably still appreciate your partner, but you might be forgetful in letting them know. Perhaps you have been together a while, and just assume that your partner is aware. However, being vocal about your appreciation is great for maintaining positivity and love in the relationship.

These conversations are simple and make both individuals feel good about the relationship. These conversations can be about anything, from chores around the house to their eyes.

It is simple to tell your partner, "I really appreciate it when you do the dishes before I get back from work. I love how much you make my life easier," or "I really appreciate your support when I am in a bad mood. You always cheer me up, and I know that I can count on you."

Sharing these words between you reminds you both of what you have together. When was the last time you said something like this to your partner? Perhaps set a goal of saying an appreciative sentence to your significant other at least once a day. You will be shocked at how little things like this can strengthen and grow a relationship.

ROUTINE CONVERSATIONS

Life is not just about declaring your love and appreciation for your significant other though. There are also just simple conversations about routine and daily tasks, things that we need to achieve and chores to be done.

These conversations don't often make you feel loved by your partner; "Hey can you vacuum the stairs," is not a sentence that fills you with great romance. But, these conversations are necessary when in a partnership.

In making these conversations constructive and not destructive, it is important to remember your tone of voice. Most of what we take from a conversation comes from tone of voice and body language and not what is actually said, therefore it is necessary to be mindful of these things when having routine conversations with your partner. If we ignore how we say things, this can lead to conflict and tension in the relationship.

Also remember to be appreciative when having these conversations. Thank your partner for helping out with chores of childcare. Remind them of what they are good at. Remind them that you love them. A "thank you, I love you," and a kiss on the cheek after every routine conversation keeps the respect and love alive.

CONVERSATIONS TO DISCOVER

When you are with someone for a long time, you think you know everything about them. You think that there are no more conversations to be had about their life, past and future dreams. This is, mostly, wrong. You will never know every single thing about your partner and there are still conversations to be had to allow you to discover and understand each other more.

A successful relationship means that you are best friends. Sometimes as relationships progress, you stop telling them things that you did at the beginning. You might think that a funny story that happened to you once is boring and shouldn't be shared. But, it most certainly should be. Childhood memories, old dating stories and family history are all things to discuss and discover about one another. You may think you know each other inside out, but there still will be things to discover no matter how long you have been together!

Have you ever talked about

- The job you wanted as a child?
- Your first pet?
- Your most embarrassing teenage story?
- Who your grandparents were?
- Your favorite subject at school?

These things might sound unimportant, but in learning more about your partner every day, or month or year, means that you will carry on falling in love with each other and strengthening the bond you have.

Certain types of conversations might feel necessary at the time, but are in fact extremely destructive for a relationship and sows the seeds for turning the relationship toxic. It is important to be aware of these types of conversations and keep them in mind when talking to your partner.

NAGGING

Sometimes you need your partner to do something or behave in a certain way. Perhaps chores around the house need to be done, or your parents are coming to visit so you are asking your partner to not swear as much. These are necessary conversations to have as a relationship is about balance and helping one another in life. However, these conversations run the risk of becoming nagging, and this can ruin even the healthiest of relationships.

Nagging is when someone constantly is asking or urging someone else to do things. The main problem with nagging is that it never really works. The person being nagged feels defensive and doesn't want to do what is asked. Which is understandable! Nobody likes getting nagged! However, people who nag often don't realize they are doing it. This creates major disharmony in the relationship and can turn toxic quickly.

Signs that you are nagging include if you are asking your partner to do something several times. You may ask them to take the garbage out, and in a few hours repeat the request. This makes your partner feel attacked and under pressure, when actually taking the garbage out is simple and they probably will get around to doing it! A good way to avoid nagging and get your partner to take the garbage out is to, after asking them to take the bins out twice, give them words of encouragement and focus on what they do around the house that makes you feel good! It sounds silly, and you might not want to, but focusing on what your partner is doing right and not what they are doing wrong is a great way to maintain positivity in the relationship and avoid nagging.

Another sign that you are nagging your partner is if you feel helpless in the situation. Perhaps you start to feel that your partner is never going to take the garbage out and that they will never listen to your requests ever again. Know that this isn't true. Focus on what you can do to help the situation. When you find yourself nagging about chores, remind yourself that your relationship is more important than this and tell your partner "Let's do this together." Yes, taking the garbage out is a one person job, but a relationship is about helping one another out. Go from "Can you take the garbage out," to, "Shall we take the garbage out together?" This allows your partner to realize that you have a request and also allows you to work together in your relationship.

TRYING TO ALWAYS BE RIGHT

How many times have you heard someone on the TV or in person say that their significant other always "has to be right"? This is a common complaint in marriages and relationships, the idea that one of the individuals involved always needs to win the argument. This is not healthy and can be extremely destructive in a relationship!

It is normal to want to always be right, but it is not normal to not be able to admit when you are in the wrong. If both parties in the couple need to be right, then the problems that occur in the relationship will never be resolved, therefore ultimately destroying the relationship.

So, how do we know when to admit we are in the wrong? Firstly, take a step back from the conversation. Go spend time alone to think things through. Imagine yourself in your partner's shoes and try to see things from their perspective. How did they say they felt? What facts did they provide to back their points up?

Now, look at if there is any common ground in what the conversation is about. If you have found some, go back to your partner and tell them. Also look at the possible outcomes of the conversation and if the disagreement is necessary. Right and wrong is really a matter of opinion and it is helpful to be aware of this.

Sally has a new friend at work, Jeff. Jeff invites Sally for drinks and sends her funny emails. Her partner Hamza thinks that Jeff is interested in Sally in a romantic way and this causes heated discussions in the relationship. Hamza and Sally are comfortable in their relationship and know that neither of them would cheat, but Hamza is annoyed at how Sally seems oblivious to Jeff's intentions. Sally thinks that Jeff is only trying to be nice. Both Hamza and Sally believe that they are right.

In order to work through this issue, both individuals need to firstly step back and see things from their partner's perspective. Sally needs to see that Hamza is feeling slightly insecure and worried. Hamza needs to see that for Sally, her and Jeff are just friends and he should not dictate who Sally is friends with.

From then, they can talk about if there is any common ground. They both love each other and would not cheat. They both agree that Sally does not see Jeff in a romantic way. They can agree on this in the conversation. Now, they need to look at the possible outcomes. If this becomes an issue in their relationship, it may turn toxic. Neither of them wants this. They need to both admit that they are both right, but also both wrong. It is only natural for Hamza to feel insecure and threatened, but he must realize that he cannot tell Sally who she can and can't be friends with. Sally needs to know that she can be friends with whoever she wants, but needs to understand how this might affect Hamza. In admitting these things, the couple can work to move on from this issue.

CHAPTER 5
BEYOND THE CONVERSATION

Learning how to communicate in a supportive and healthy way with your partner is the foundation for a long lasting and enjoyable relationship. However, in order to truly gain the most out of your relationship, you must learn beyond the conversation. It is great to talk about things, but there is more to a relationship than just talking. For a relationship to last a lifetime, we need to be able to show our love to our partners and be conscious of our actions.

The French poet Pierre Reverdy once said, "There is no love, there are only proofs of love." Whatever love that we feel towards someone is ultimately meaningless unless we do things to show and prove our love.

This is especially important when a relationship has evolved past the honeymoon phase. The grind of everyday life, work, children, chores and family commitments all have an impact on our relationship. You might not forget to say "I love you" to your partner when they go to work or when you hang up the phone, but after a while this phrase might feel meaningless and more of a habit than any actual declaration of love. In order to keep the love alive, both people in the relationship need to be aware of body language and actions that they do both intentionally and unintentionally.

INTENTIONAL ACTIONS

We have all heard the phrase, "Actions speak louder than words." This is true in regard to most things in life, but especially true in relationships. We can say we love, respect and support our partner until we are blue in the face, but it all comes down to our actions. We all have been there for a friend who is in an unhealthy relationship, and witnessed how words can be meaningless. Your friend might say that her boyfriend cheated on her, or stood her up on a date. He might then apologize, and tell her that he loves her. But, this is meaningless. His actions have not proved his love to her, therefore the words that he is saying do not matter. Similarly, someone might feel unsupported by their partner even if they claim to be supportive. Telling your partner, "I support you in your goal to be an artist," is meaningless if you do not look at their art and attend galleries with them.

In order to make a relationship work, we need to back up our love with intentional actions.

USING LOVE LANGUAGES

Think back to the five love languages. Four out of five love languages rely on actions rather than words, showing that these are very important in a relationship. Using these can really improve a relationship and show your partner that you love them.

Jane and Becky did an online test for their love languages. Both had words of affirmation as their most important one, and therefore they took it upon themselves to be vocal about their love and support for one another. It has helped the relationship, however Becky feels that there is still something lacking and wants Jane to show her more love in different ways.

She retakes the love language test and words of affirmation came out on top again, but she looks at her second love language. She sees it is physical touch. She tells Jane this and suggests that actions are also important in their relationship. They build on this, using physical touch to show each other their love.

Their situation shows that even if your love language is words of affirmation, it is important to pay attention to the others. Words are important for most couples, but a balance between actions and words can maintain a fair and loving relationship. Showing your love might make your partner feel ten times more loved than simply telling them.

PAYING ATTENTION

How often do you feel your partner is not listening to you? This is a common complaint in couples that have been together for a while. However, it does not mean that your partner is not listening. When you are used to each other and know each other well, you become more in tune to their thoughts and feelings. This might mean that you find it easy to only half listen to what they are saying, as you know their train of thought and how they react to certain situations. But, this can become an issue in a relationship. There is no malice or bad intentions in this, but it can create feelings of resentment and sadness. Your partner might not feel you love them as much as you once did. They might worry that they bore you and that is not fair to them.

However, we are able to use our actions to show that we are really paying attention to our partners. When you are sitting on the sofa and talking with your partner, turn towards them to show that you are paying attention. Put a hand on their leg, maintain eye contact. Nods and words of encouragement or agreement can help let your partner know that you are listening to them. In paying attention to your partner, you are showing your love to them using both conversational and physical tools.

Paying attention is not just about showing you are listening to them. You can also use other actions to give your partner attention and show that you love them. Giving your partner attention in a physical yet non-sexual way is a great and easy way to pay attention to them. Hand holding is the perfect and most simple way of providing a physical action that shows love and support. Closeness and cuddles on the sofa in front of TV can be both relaxing and supportive.

Figure 8

When out shopping, an arm around your partner when browsing the aisles is another small but effective way of showing love.

Remember Jane and Becky whose love language was both words of affirmation. During the time they were discovering and discussing their love languages, Becky had been laid-off and was looking for a job. This had affected her self esteem and self worth, and Jane, knowing that her love language was words of affirmation, told Becky multiple times a day that she was great, smart and a hard worker. She told her that she will soon find a new job.

UNINTENTIONAL ACTIONS

We have looked at intentional actions as ways to support our partners, but we also need to be aware of unintentional actions that can have detrimental effects on our relationships. We may be telling our partners we love them, but have actions that suggest otherwise. These actions are not intentional, but still push your partner away. It is vital to be aware of body language and physical space in a relationship. In knowing these things, you can avoid unnecessary conflict.

BODY LANGUAGE

Body language is the language all humans speak. Energy and attitude comes from the way we hold ourselves and negative body language can make or break a relationship. Most communication really does come from our body language as we use our bodies to convey meaning and emotion.

Imagine sitting on the sofa with your partner. You are hunched away from them, arms folded, looking the opposite way. You say, "I love you." Do you expect your partner to feel loved? Now picture you sitting on the sofa with them but in this instance you are turned towards your partner, an arm around their shoulders, gazing into their eyes. You say, "I love you."

In both instances you have said the exact same thing, but the meaning is completely different. This is solely because of your body language. For your relationship to be long-lasting and strong, you need to be aware of your body language and what it is telling your partner.

Most body language we use is unintentional. We do not realize that our bodies are telling our partners what we are really feeling, even if our mouths are saying something different. We might also mean what we are telling our partners, but our bodies are not in tune with our thoughts. A lot of the time this is in reaction to previous relationships. We learn body language through other people and take this on without meaning to. A woman who has been frightened of a previous partner is more likely to use closed-off body language to their current partner. She probably does not mean to do this, but it has a negative impact on her current relationship.

Body language can start off as a reaction to something small, but can grow to become a serious issue in the relationship. The energy and vibes that come from our bodies can linger and be repeated. It is, therefore, necessary to be aware of our unintentional body language and be active in changing it.

A waitress in a busy restaurant is passing the time by polishing glasses and watching couples eating their meals. She enjoys this part of the job, watching romance blossom. She can easily tell who is on their first date, their second date or their fiftieth. The restaurant is quite loud, with music playing, people chattering and clanging and shouting coming from the kitchen. This means that she can't really hear what is being said on each table in the restaurant, but she can watch them. She has soon learnt that watching people's body language tells her more about them than eavesdropping into conversations.

There are two tables by the window and each table has a couple sitting down and enjoying their meal. She watches them. The couple on the left are leaning over the table to each other. Their hands are on the table and occasionally brush against one another. They are gazing into each other's eyes, and the waitress even notices the woman resting her feet against the man's leg underneath the table. They seem oblivious to the rest of the restaurant, only looking away from each other to order or thank the waitress for their food.

The couple on the right has a completely different energy. The man is sitting back from the table, his arms folded, staring down to his plate. The woman is gazing around the restaurant, picking at her food, her arms and legs tucked in towards her body.

Both couples have completely different body languages and the waitress can understand their situations so clearly, even though the only words she has heard them say is when they ordered their food. Now, next time you are at a restaurant with your significant other, try and think about which couple you are, the one on the left or the one on the right? The waitress assumed the couple on the left had only just started dating, but she was, for the first time, wrong! This couple had been dating twice as long as the couple on the right, and they were out to celebrate their twentieth wedding anniversary. They, however, knew the importance of body language to show each other their love. It is not only the honeymooners that can be all gooey and romantic!

If you and your partner are more like the couple on the right, your relationship isn't doomed. It just needs some work. If you realize you are sitting apart from each other at the restaurant, try and lean in. Put your hand across the table and take your partner's. Touch your foot against their leg. Don't look around the restaurant; give your partner your full attention. Conveying your love to your partner in these ways will help solidify and protect your relationship.

TURN TOWARD EACH OTHER INSTEAD OF AWAY

The psychologist and researcher John Gottman proposed that there are seven principles for making a marriage work. In his book he discusses and promotes these seven ways that guide you and your partner to a supportive and healthy relationship.

The third principle suggests that when in conversation with a partner, turning away from each other can have negative impacts on the relationship. One of the drawbacks of a long-lasting relationship is that we take our partner for granted. This is because we are aware of our love, but sometimes forget to show it. This is mostly unintentional, and because of our comfort in our relationship, we might turn away from them instead of toward them.

Gottman suggests that in every relationship there are "bids" for each other's attention. The partner then responds to the bid by either turning toward them or turning away. Romance and love is kept alive when we turn toward our partner. It builds on the trust and support the relationship is built on and reminds both parties that they are in the right relationship.

It is evening time and Mike has just got home from work. His wife Azami is in the kitchen preparing dinner. She is cooking pasta with a tomato sauce and calls through to Mike when he arrives home. He comes into the kitchen to get a beer.

"Shall I grate some cheese for the pasta?" she asks him. Mike grunts and shrugs, opening his beer and not looking at his wife. Here, he has turned away from Azami, not toward her. This is obviously upsetting for her, and she feels angry and unloved. Mike does love her, but he takes her for granted.

Because of these situations and Mike repeatedly turning away, Azami needed space and went to stay with her sister for the weekend. He is confused, as he loves her and used to tell her every night before bed. He would cuddle up to her on the sofa and hold her hand when out for walks. But, he has unintentionally pushed his wife away time and time again, and these little things can create great conflict in a relationship.

In this situation, Mike should have turned towards his wife. It is as simple as him looking at her, giving her a kiss on the cheek and saying that he appreciates her cooking dinner.

According to Gottman, most arguments between couples are not about specific topics like money or sex, but rather from failed bids. These little things that seem unimportant can make or break a relationship. It is crucial to be aware of these bids for affection from your partner and to not unintentionally turn away from them. In turning toward them, you are keeping the romance alive and building a stronger connection every single day.

CHAPTER 6
COMMUNICATION AND SEX

Communication is the foundation for a healthy relationship and this includes communicating about sex. However, even the happiest and most stable couples can find it hard to talk about sex. Taboos or embarrassment that are caused by society can affect an individual's confidence in discussing these things. But we need to remember, sex is why we are all here! It is natural and beautiful and can be very fun.

In order to create a fulfilling and supportive sexual partnership between you and your significant other, being open and honest about sex is key. Try and forget taboos, and tell yourself that sex is the most natural thing and we are built to enjoy it! Before we can get down to it, though, we should have conversations with our partners about sex. Consent, power and health are all important and should not be ignored. There is no "ruining the mood" when it comes to these conversations, rather they build a strong foundation for sexual health and wellbeing.

NECESSARY CONVERSATIONS

Some things regarding sex need to be communicated and if they aren't, we run the risk of damaging our health and happiness. In regard to a sexual relationship, you must remember that your individual choices and own health and wellbeing are more important than pleasing your partner. Not talking about certain things can seriously damage both yours and your partner's mental and physical health. But, talking about these things doesn't always have to be hard. When approached in a respectful and calm manner, we can fully understand one another sexually.

SEXUAL HEALTH

Discussing sexual health with your significant other, or someone you are going to be sexually intimate with, can feel awkward and unnecessary. You might feel that it is easier to not talk about it, but avoiding the conversation can have serious implications on you and your partner's health and trust.

Common sexually transmitted diseases such as chlamydia and gonorrhea can damage your fertility, and according to the Center for Disease Control and Prevention, about one in seven individuals living in the USA with HIV do not know they have it. It can be a scary topic to approach, but a little bit of awkwardness is much better than infecting your partner, or getting infected, with a sexually transmitted disease.

Knowing your body and its sexual health can ease anxiety and help you relax in regard to sex. In talking about it with your partner, you are showing that you care, and this can help you get closer emotionally. Bringing up getting tested doesn't have to be too awkward and there are ways to do it in a friendly and relaxed manner. Think about going to the sexual health clinic in the same way you go to the dentist. It is not embarrassing to make sure your teeth are healthy, so why should we be embarrassed about making sure our sexual organs are healthy?

When approaching the subject with your partner, try to be relaxed. Start off by saying, "I love you, I really enjoy our sex life, but I just thought, when was the last time you got tested? Maybe we should go together." Remember this is not about not trusting your partner, and make sure they know this. STIs are so common and sneaky and many people don't realize they have them!

Getting tested together means you can support each other and be open about sex. This is great and can be a bonding experience with your partner. If your partner does not want to get tested, this is really a red flag for your relationship and you must ask yourself why they are not wanting to get tested. Perhaps it is merely embarrassment, but it could be something worse. Furthermore, it shows they have a disregard for their health and yours. Either way, it is something that must be addressed.

CONTRACEPTION

In a similar vein, contraception is something that is often not communicated in a relationship as there is a belief that it will kill the mood. But, what really kills the mood is an unplanned pregnancy! When getting in a sexual relationship with someone, it is necessary to be aware that sex can lead to pregnancy. If you and your partner are not ready for that yet, you need to put things in place to lessen the chances of it occurring.

This may sound obvious, you are a grown-up, and you know these things. But, surprisingly even the smartest and confident people can lapse judgment when it comes to contraception.

Firstly, if you and your partner have not been tested for STIs, you need to use a condom. Other forms of birth control do not protect against STIs. If you have both been tested, then you can have the discussion of moving on to a different type of contraception. Remember that birth control is a responsibility for both individuals in a relationship, not just the woman. In being open and communicative about these things, you can make sure that you are both on the same page. Men should be able to ask their significant other about birth control and women should be able to tell their partner if they want to change it or come off it. For a lot of people, trying out birth control and finding the right one can take time. It is important to be willing to take this time and be safe and respectful.

PLEASURE

Sex is about pleasure and connecting with your significant other. It is important to take the time to discuss pleasure with your partner when not in the bedroom. Do not talk about pleasure before or after sex, as this can make things awkward or make it seem like you are critical of the sex.

Figure 9

Start the discussion regarding pleasure when you are both relaxed and comfortable. Perhaps after dinner when you have sat on the sofa to watch TV. Pour a glass of wine or a coffee, turn to your partner and ask them if you can have a talk about your sex life and pleasure. Are you enjoying what is going on? Do you want to have more foreplay?

It is important to talk about yourself and your feelings and pleasure, and not put blame or criticism onto your partner. For example, instead of saying, "You don't touch my nipples enough," say "I would like it if you started to touch my nipples more." Remember, nobody should be doing anything they do not wish to do, and it is about finding out what you both enjoy and want to do. You do not owe your partner anything sexually, and they do not owe you anything sexually.

It is important to remember that pleasure can change over time. What you enjoyed when you first got together with your partner might not be the same as after you have been together for ten years. Do not feel like you can't talk about this change! It is healthy for our interests to develop and alter over time, and tell your partner this. They might be feeling the same, too, and just not feeling comfortable about bringing it up.

DIFFERENCES

In being open and communicative with your partner in regard to sex, you must be open about your differences. If you feel pressured into doing something you don't like sexually with your partner, this is a red flag and you must remove yourself from the situation. Be aware of consent and boundaries.

Remember, just because you are in a sexual relationship with your long term partner, doesn't mean that consent is always given. You do not owe them anything and they do not owe you anything.

Sexual likes and dislikes are complex and varied. In building a strong and healthy sexual relationship with your partner, you should be able to freely discuss these things. Talk about what you love, and ask them what they love. Identify sexual similarities and differences. In doing this, you are strengthening your relationship and allowing for a fulfilling and beautiful sex life.

SIGNS OF AN UNHEALTHY SEXUAL RELATIONSHIP

In building an open, healthy and communicative sexual relationship, you must be aware of signs of an unhealthy one. In knowing the sexual warning signs and red flags, we can know when to end a relationship, or when to remove sex from the equation.

NOT TALKING

Sometimes individuals find it difficult to talk about sex openly and honestly. This can be caused by a myriad of factors but is most often caused by embarrassment or insecurity. Kate's boyfriend John is lovely. Their dating is going well, he keeps the romance alive by picking her flowers or taking her out to dinner. She equally shows her love to him through words and actions. They talk about everything, from their hopes and dreams to their deepest fears. Kate knows all about John's passions and John knows all about Kate's idyllic childhood. Their relationship is perfect, nearly.

There is one thing they struggle to talk about, and that is sex. Kate finds the sex boring and does not feel fulfilled in the relationship. However, every time she attempts to bring it up, John gets embarrassed and shuts Kate out.

This is a sign of an unhealthy sexual relationship. In not talking about their differences, wants and needs, they are struggling to fully commit to each other. So what should Kate do?

This is difficult for both parties and both individuals involved need to see things from their partners perspective. It is unfair that Kate is not sexually fulfilled, and John needs to understand this. However, Kate needs to be aware that there are reasons that John might be unwilling to talk. There might be reasons in John's past that makes him feel insecure about his sexuality, and he might feel overwhelmed by the pressure that society puts on both men and women sexually.

For John and Kate, if they do not address this problem their relationship is doomed. But Kate needs to address this issue in the correct way. She must use "I feel" statements and not accuse John of anything. Before approaching the topic of sex, she could also show John support by telling him all the things that he is doing correctly.

If John is still unable to talk, removing sex from the relationship might be the best option in order to protect Kate's sexual wellbeing. This is not to punish John, but rather a safeguarding technique to protect and ensure bodily autonomy and a healthy attitude toward sex.

TALKING ABOUT THE PAST

Another sign of an unhealthy sexual relationship is bringing up the past. This can be in regard to past sexual partners or experiences that either you or your partner have had. It is healthy and perhaps a relationship strengthening conversation to discuss past sexual partners or experiences, but if these things are constantly brought up in the current relationship, this is unhealthy and a cause of conflict. People cannot change the past, so if you cannot accept your partner's past then that is not accepting them as an autonomous person and will constantly cause conflict in your relationship.

Unfortunately, there is a stigma in regard to how many sexual partners a woman has had. Without realizing it, people can internalize this stigma and project it onto their partners. There is nothing wrong with sex and there should be no shame attached to the number of people you have had sex with. If your partner brings this up in conflict or in conversation, you must address this. It should not be used as ammunition in an argument.

Furthermore, if you or your significant other compare each other sexually to past partners, you must look at why you are doing it. Are you unfulfilled in this relationship or are you just looking at ways to hurt your current partner? Either way, it is incredibly harmful and destructive.

It is okay to recognize sexual habits from previous relationships when discussing your wants and needs, but never tell your partner that your ex used to do a certain thing and you miss that. Rather, tell them that you would enjoy that certain thing. If you are constantly thinking, "This is not as good as it was with my ex," then you really need to address the sexual problems in your current relationship.

Remember, not all relationships are the same and therefore each one brings with it a new way to connect and new things to explore. This is exciting and wonderful, and therefore do not fixate on the past and your pleasure with past lovers. Focus on the now, and how this one is different and the ways in which it is better. Work on how to fix the sexual differences you have and this is down to communicating fairly with your partner.

Let go of the past and focus on the present. Focus on how great your current relationship can be and put things in place to make that happen.

CONSENT

Remember that you do not owe your partner anything and they do not owe you anything. A healthy relationship means constantly being vocal about sexual boundaries and wants. If you ever feel coerced or forced by your partner, then remove yourself from the relationship. Someone who does not respect boundaries and consent is not a person that you want to be with.

Despite popular belief, there is no blurred line when it comes to consent. Just because someone is your partner does not mean they consent. Just because someone has consented before does not mean they are in the current situation. A sexual relationship requires constant and vocal consent.

When having sex with your partner, it is great to be vocal about what they want and if you can do a certain thing. "Can I touch you here?" or, "Do you want me to lick you here?" and similar sentences are great in order to have a fun and healthy sexual encounter with your partner.

In regard to consent, it must be freely given and given with enthusiasm. When it comes to sex, you should only do things you want to do. This means that there should be no obligations or expectations in a sexual relationship. Furthermore, consent is reversible. People should be able to change their mind and be vocal about such change. If an individual feels scared or unsafe to withdraw consent, this is a red flag and therefore means that the relationship is toxic.

Any signs that consent is not respected in a relationship means that the relationship is harmful and you must withdraw yourself from it. If a partner has disregarded your consent, you can go to the police or health services for help and support. Rape is a crime, not a misunderstanding or the victim's fault.

Communicating about sex does not just mean the serious stuff, although the serious stuff is important! Talking about sex can also be fun and exciting, and works on the intimacy you have with your sexual partner. Intimacy can be practiced in and outside of the bedroom and sets down the foundations of a healthy and successful relationship.

Sex and intimacy is important in a relationship and often sows the seeds for a long-lasting love. Knowing and understanding each other's bodies inside and out gives you the ability to fully know your partner, nearly as much as you know yourself. Giving someone you love pleasure is one of the greatest gifts you can give them and one that connects you both to each other. However, this closeness and intimacy sometimes needs to be worked on. We need to fully know our sexual needs and be able to communicate them with our partner. Then, you can work on implementing them in your relationship.

EVALUATING YOUR SEX NEEDS

Most adults are sexual and have sexual needs. There is no shame in this, it is completely healthy. The body is made to enjoy sex and the touch of others. Sometimes it is hard to understand or evaluate what we need sexually, but taking time to explore and find out what turns us on and satisfies us means that we can fully enjoy our sexual lives.

THE ORGASM GAP

Unfortunately, there is gender inequality in the bedroom. According to durex.com, a study conducted in the Netherlands showed that up to 75% of women do not orgasm during sex. Contrastingly, only 28% of men said that they don't always climax.

There are a lot of reasons behind the orgasm gap. Some women find that their partners do not know how to press the right buttons, and that focusing solely on penetrative sex can be unhelpful in a woman achieving orgasms. For women, manual and oral stimulation of the clitoris is a great way to find pleasure.

If you are a woman and you are finding orgasms hard to achieve in your relationship, try and find out by yourself what you enjoy. Masturbating is a healthy and important part of understanding your sexuality and is just as natural for women to do as men. Take time away from your partner to explore the senses of your body and what you like and do not like. It is not your partner's fault and do not blame them for your lack of orgasm, rather take time and patience with your own sexuality to work on your confidence.

Remember, it is not bad to find orgasm difficult to achieve. You are not broken or unable to find pleasure. For women, it just might take a little bit longer to find your orgasm. Furthermore, try not to see it as the end goal to sex. Sex is about exploring pleasure, stimulation, and touch, and finding ways of expressing yourself.

Also consider the use of sex toys or stimulating lubricants to aid in the pleasure of sex. These things can seem scary and off-putting but more and more women are using sex toys such as vibrators to help them achieve orgasm with or without their partner. This is not a replacement for your partner, but rather an aid to getting the pleasure you deserve!

FINDING YOUR SEXUAL STYLE

All couples have different sexual styles that they enjoy, and this might change for a person with different sexual partners. Just because you enjoyed a certain style with one person doesn't mean you will enjoy the same in your current relationship. We tend to want and need certain things from sex, not just pleasure or orgasms. It is important to know what you want from sex and what importance you put on it.

Do you prefer sex to be more spiritual? When you see sex as a union of bodies, souls and minds you feel that sex is a spiritual event that reflects your true love and appreciation for your partner. For many people, sex is about a connection deeper than physical. If you relate to this type of sexual style, consider bringing tantric sex into your relationship. Tantric sex is about the weaving and expansion of energy, creating a connection between the mind and body. It focuses on taking sex slow and making it goal-less. According to Dr. Judy Kuriansky, in understanding tantric sex you must understand what tantra is. Tantra comes from an ancient Sanskrit language and it means 'expansion through awareness'. It is a spiritual technique that comes from ancient practices found in India, China and Nepal. It uses movement, breath and sounds to quiet the mind and activate sexual energy. Doing this can achieve states of bliss and open up energy and love for your partner and the universe. It is a meditative practice and therefore mindful, conscious of respect and honor.

If you are interested in tantric sex, take sex off the bed as this will trigger a want for sleep, meaning you might not take the sex as slow as you need. Start by lying on the floor with your partner and slowly touching each other. Take your time going over every bit of their body and experiment with the touching. Switching between light touches and stroking to more film massage heightens the senses and builds up the sensations, prolonging sex and pleasure. Inhale and exhale together in a rhythm and listen to each other's heartbeats. Remember to move and breathe slowly. Work towards a gradual build-up. There are lots of online advice and exercises in regard to tantric sex available if this is of interest to you and if your sexual type is spiritual.

You might prefer a more active and lusty style of sex, and find the joy of sex to just be about sex and bodily pleasure. This is perfectly normal too! Sex is beautiful as it is a gift to your partner of pleasure.

In thinking about what your sexual style is and what you value in sex, you are then able to implement these ideas with your partner. In knowing yourself and your individuality, you can use this knowledge to strengthen and fulfill your sexual relationship.

WE SHOULD TRY IT! ONLINE QUESTIONNAIRE

A great way in exploring and finding out your sexual needs is using questionnaires and quizzes online both by yourself and with your partner. A great one is the *We Should Try It!* questionnaire, which you do with your partner. Here, you take turns in going through sexual acts and fantasies and selecting which you are interested in trying. When you have both done the questionnaire, the website only shows sexual fantasies that you are both into.

The questionnaire varies from what type of music you wish to listen to during sex, to more obscure and extreme BDSM practices. You can just answer the basic questions and not explore the BDSM or group sex part of the questionnaire, it is entirely up to you and what you feel comfortable with.

It is great to explore topics and sexual behavior that you might be too embarrassed to bring up with your partner. As the questionnaire only shows things that both you have selected, what you have and they have not, and vice versa, is not an issue. Fantasies can seem embarrassing, but everyone has them and they are completely normal!

Exploring sexual fantasies is fun and exciting, and knowing your sexual fantasies and wants is the first step in your journey to sexual happiness. In using online quizzes, you can see what possibilities are out there to help you enjoy your sexuality.

COMMUNICATING YOUR SEX NEEDS

Once you have evaluated your sexual needs and know what you are and are not comfortable with, it is time to be open and honest about them with your partner. It is important to remember to be honest and kind when discussing sex with your significant other. You should never say things that border on criticism and remember to ask your partner rather than tell them.

BE POSITIVE

When approaching the topic of your sexual needs, remember to do it in a neutral place. Never do it before or after sex or in the bedroom. Do not dance around the topic, be upfront and honest about what it is that you wish to discuss. Your sex life is not just about you, but you and your partner. In order to have productive and communicative discussions about your sexual needs, remember to be positive! If you wish your partner to go down on you more, never say things like, "You don't go down on me enough," as that is accusatory and harmful. Tell your partner that you would like them to go down on you more, but remember that they do not owe you anything.

A great way of keeping the conversation friendly and kind is to be positive. Start by telling your partner things that they do that you like. Always say something positive before asking or suggesting things. This way you can build on what you enjoy in your relationship and find ways of improving.

Perhaps you are finding it hard to get the conversation going. Certain things are necessary to discuss when it comes to sexual satisfaction and addressing these particular topics is a great way to be specific and productive in the conversation. When talking about your sexual needs with your partner, go through these questions:

- Comfort - Firstly, ask one another if there is anything either of you do or have done that is uncomfortable for the other. Your partner might do something that they think you enjoy, however you don't. It is necessary to be open and honest with your partner about your likes and dislikes. It is important not to be in discomfort just because your partner wants something sexually.

- Time - How do you both feel about how often you are having sex? Do either of you feel like you are having sex too much or too little? Not feeling like you do not have enough time for sex because of work or family commitments can put a strain on your relationship and it is important to address these issues before it becomes a problem. Remember, as long as you are discussing things in a respectful and calm manner you are building on your relationship. Think about what you and your partner can do to make time for sexual intimacy. Perhaps there are certain events in your schedule that you could forgo in order to give you and your partner quality time together.

- Changes - Are there any changes both physically and emotionally that might be affecting your sex life? Illness or weight gain can impact a person's self-esteem and therefore their relationship with their partner. You might not feel as confident as you once did and need reassurance and support from your partner. Sometimes all that is needed is a few kind words of encouragement.

- Emotions - Are you getting enough emotional support? If you start to feel that your partner is not there emotionally, your desire for sex might be affected. It is great to make sure you and your partner have a strong emotional bond before attempting to fix your sex life.

BREAKING THE ROUTINE

Perhaps you and your partner have found sex to be too monotonous and predictable. For some couples, sex becomes part of the daily list of chores to complete. This does not mean that your sex life is over! Rather, it means that you might need to put in a little bit extra work to spice things up. Remember, your sex life is just as important as your work or family life!

Sometimes spicing your sex life up means going back to the basics. When was the last time you cuddled and kissed? Sitting or lying down and stoking each other is a great way to work on intimacy and your sex life. This helps to build up the eroticism and remind you both of how exciting sex is. Couples that have been together for a while run the risk of forgetting the kissing, but kissing is great for bonding and enhancing emotional and physical intimacy. Perhaps spend an evening just kissing! It might lead to sex, or might not, but try and make kissing, not sex, the goal one evening.

Sex is not a race to the finish! You need to take your time to engage emotionally and physically with your partner. It can be hard to fully immerse yourself in sex when you live hectic and busy lives, but try and remember that sex is just as important as everything else. When in doubt, take things slower. Explore every inch of your partner's body.

Other ways of breaking up the routine can be bringing new things into your sex life. There is a huge range of products to help you spice things up in the bedroom which you can buy online or in a store. When it comes to vibrators, there are so many different ones to try! A great starting point are bullet vibrators. These are small and can be purchased quite cheaply and are designed for clitoral stimulation. More and more couples are incorporating vibrators into their sex lives to enhance pleasure. Outfits and lingerie are also great ways of breaking out of the routine. These things can also help you love your body and remind you that you are a sexual being with needs! Sex board or card games can also be purchased to add a little spice into things.

Watching movies and reading books can also be helpful in discovering new ideas. Watching porn together can be fun, but also there are a vast range of erotic and soft porn films to discover. Some of these can be watched on major film and TV streaming platforms and can both get you in the mood and give you fun ideas to try.

Have sex in somewhere other than the bedroom is another extremely fun way of breaking the routine. Talk to your partner about different places to experiment in. You won't be disappointed!

These are just a few ways of breaking the routine. Go through these as a couple and discuss what you might fancy trying. Be open and honest and don't shy away from talking about what you might be interested in!

FANTASIES

Sexual fantasies are completely normal and a natural part of a person's sexuality. Everyone has fantasies and they should not be a source of embarrassment! However, sometimes we find it hard to discuss our sexual fantasies with our partners.

Is it great to first figure out your goal in discussing your sexual fantasies. Do you want to try them out? Do you want to watch porn or talk dirty about your fantasy? In knowing what you want from the discussion, you might find it easier to discuss. First, remind yourself and your partner that there is no pressure on trying out your sexual fantasies. Make sure your partner knows that it is completely fine if it isn't their cup of tea. Maybe start the conversation with more vanilla fantasies before explaining your more extreme ones. This gets the ball rolling and allows your partner to open up about their own fantasies.

After telling your partner your fantasy, let your partner guide the conversation. They might want to change the topic, or they might want to discuss it further. They might need to take time to figure out if they are interested in trying it out. Be aware that they might react negatively, but do not feel ashamed of sharing your fantasy. Remember that fantasies aren't gross or creepy and they are natural. Everyone has them and your partner probably does too! Fantasies are a way of expressing subconscious desires and exploring your sexuality.

If you and your partner are still finding the topic of fantasies hard to approach, perhaps try a little game to aid the discussion. Get a hat or bowl and scraps of paper. Both you and your partner then write down different fantasies on the scraps of paper, and put them in the hat. These can be things as simple as different sex positions, or more extreme fantasies. Then take turns unfolding the paper. Read the fantasy and try to discuss them. This eases the initial embarrassment and can be a great bonding game for you and your partner!

CHAPTER 8
KEEPING THE LOVE ALIVE

The honeymoon phase always ends right? We stop falling in love and focus on just being in a relationship? Things get in the way and real life takes over? Well, this doesn't have to be the case! There are ways of making the honeymoon phase last an entire relationship!

Falling in love can last forever. It's a common misconception that love fades and if we have the right tools we can keep the love alive. It doesn't even have to be hard work, it can be about little things that remind each other of your love; romantic acts, spontaneity, or meditation on your love. This chapter will explore the ways that you and your partner can consistently keep the love alive so the honeymoon phase is always there.

THE SEVEN PRINCIPLES OF MAKING MARRIAGE WORK

A great way of keeping the love alive is to return to John Gottman's seven principles of making a marriage work. Here, the psychologist and researcher puts forward principles and ideas to enhance and maintain romance in your relationship. These ideas are simple and effective and will give you and your partner tools to keep your love alive. At its core, Gottman's seven principles are about having a deep friendship with your partner. In knowing your partner intimately, you create a great and strong bond that will last a lifetime.

LOVE MAPS

This principle suggests that happy couples have love maps of each other. These love maps are knowledge about one another, such as likes and dislikes, dreams and goals. Constantly finding out more and more details about your partner's life such as the name of their boss or favorite film means that you can try to understand them fully. In understanding your partner more, you can love them deeply.

Ways to enhance your love maps are making sure you sit down and talk to your partner about anything and everything. Make your partner your priority and ask them questions you might not have asked them before.

Figure 10

Imagine a couple, John and Sandra. They have been together for about five years and have lived together for the last few. They enjoy each other's company and have fun together, and their sex is great. However, Sandra thinks there is something missing.

Sandra always remembers to set John's favorite TV show to record if she knows John will miss it. She can name all of John's work colleagues and friends. John, however, does not even know the name of Sandra's brother. John doesn't think it's a big deal, because he is dating Sandra not Sandra's brother! But, the fact he is dating Sandra is exactly why he needs to know the name of her brother. Sandra's love map of John is detailed, but John's love map of Sandra is not. This causes friction in the relationship. Even though they live together and spend so much time together, Sandra feels that John doesn't really even know her. She can't explain why, but she feels sad about their relationship.

In order to keep the loved alive, John needs to work on enhancing his love map. Remember, there are always things to discover about your partner! John and Sandra decide to go out on a date once a week and take this time to discover more about each other. Doing this helps the couple feel more and more connected, making the love between them grow.

NURTURE YOUR FONDNESS AND ADMIRATION

Fondness and admiration for each other are the two most crucial factors in making a relationship strong, stable and long-lasting. It is fine to acknowledge your partner's personal flaws, but you can do this with fondness and admiration.

Think back to your first dates with your partner. What was it about them that made you fall in love? Their humor? The way they laughed? These things are still there and to keep the love alive, you need to remind yourself of how great your partner is.

A great way of doing this is both you and your partner writing down three things about each other that you love. Perhaps they are kind and caring? Courageous and smart? Now think of ways recently that your partner has shown you these characteristics. Remind yourself that this is why you love them and they are the same person from your first date. Meditate on your fondness for your partner and make sure you are aware of how much you appreciate them. This helps to reignite the romance in your relationship, heading it back to the honeymoon phase.

TURNING TOWARD EACH OTHER INSTEAD OF AWAY

This principle has been mentioned before in this book. It is about the little things in the relationship we do and our body language towards our partner. To be a happy couple you need to be open with your partner, giving them your full attention. Little moments of connection solidify love and keep the romance alive. The beauty of this principle is that once you are aware of it, it is so easily done.

In order to turn toward each other and not away, you need to be aware of the distractions in the world. The internet, phones and TV can all get in the way of turning toward your partner. Perhaps when your partner returns home from work you are watching TV so don't fully welcome them back. Electronic devices have meant that distraction has now become a habit and this has negative consequences on modern relationships. Checking phones and answering emails are all small ways that mean that you don't fully turn toward your partner. However, to keep the love alive, it is important to be present with your partner. Next time they get home from work and you are watching TV, switch it off and turn to your partner. Ask them how their day is going and turn toward them instead of away.

LET YOUR PARTNER INFLUENCE YOU

This principle suggests that happy couples keep the love alive by working as a team. In order to be in a successful and romantic relationship, it is important to consider each other's opinions and beliefs. It is important to listen to each other and let the other person influence them. This leads to making decisions as a couple and a team, not as an individual.

Gottman suggests that men are less likely to listen to their partner's advice and influence in a relationship. This causes strain and upset in the relationship as the other person might feel ignored and pushed out. This principle is a lot to do with understanding and communication and building a life together, not apart.

Imagine James and David have recently both booked time off work. They want to do something as a couple but haven't decided what. James wants to go to the seaside for a few days but David just wants to relax at home. This can cause friction in the relationship, but if they both open up and let each other influence them then they can work on being happy and enjoying their time off together.

In order for them to follow this principle they need to listen to each other and understand each other's point of view. In doing this they can show empathy and avoid criticizing each other. Perhaps David has been feeling really stressed and anxious recently and just wants to be in the comfort of his own home. Maybe James knows David is stressed and believes that a few days away will be helpful. However, whatever decision they come to, they must let each other influence them. This will strengthen their relationship and their communicating skills.

SOLVE YOUR SOLVABLE PROBLEMS

Gottman identifies two types of problems in a relationship, solvable and perpetual ones. Perpetual ones are to do with big issues and solvable problems normally feel less intense and situational. Working on these solvable problems using empathy and other techniques learnt in previous chapters means that you can focus on keeping the romance alive in your relationship instead of bickering about chores or schedule.

OVERCOMING GRIDLOCK

Unfortunately, many couples face gridlock when it comes to their perpetual problems. This is when neither partner can adapt and accept to overcome their perpetual problems. Gottman suggests that gridlock is a sign that there are dreams and beliefs that your partner isn't aware of. In order to overcome this, it is necessary to acknowledge and accept our partner's dreams. You both need to be aware that one dream is not better or worse than another, but that because of your upbringing and early life, your dreams and goals differ.

Every relationship will find themselves gridlocked at one point or another. But, finding ways around this can strengthen your relationship. Every individual is their own person and has their own views and beliefs. In order to keep the love alive, you must acknowledge your partner's dreams and learn to access and accept them in your own way.

CREATE SHARED MEANING

When couples create shared meaning together they are building on their love, making it long-lasting and enriched. Gottman suggests that marriage and relationships are not just about living together, raising children and splitting chores. Rather, there is a deeper and more spiritual side to relationships that often gets overlooked. In creating shared meaning, you are creating a rich inner life full of symbols and rituals. These things create an intense bond between you and your partner and mean the honeymoon phase will last forever.

Gottman laid out four pillars that allow you and your partner to create shared meaning. The first is rituals of connection. In setting out rituals of connection in your relationship, you are reinforcing your bond. These rituals can be little things, such as sharing a coffee in bed every morning, but can also be things like spending each Christmas on holiday by the sea. Rituals develop naturally but it is important to carry them on in your relationship to keep your love and connection alive.

The second pillar is about support for each other's roles. In a couple, it is good to be aware of the role both ourselves and our partners play in the relationship. In recognizing the roles and knowing what we expect from our partner, we can support each other in this.

The third pillar is regarding shared goals. Think about what both you and your partner want out of life and identify shared goals. When identified, discuss with your partner ways to work toward these goals. In doing this, your bond and intimacy will flourish, creating new meaning for your relationship.

The last pillar is shared values and symbols. These regard philosophical, ethical and religious beliefs on how you wish to lead your life. Identifying shared belief systems in your relationship bonds you together and creates a deeper love for each other. Symbols and objects you share together can have meaning. Perhaps there is a piece of furniture in your house that you got when you moved in together? Or a necklace that your partner bought for you in the early days of your relationship? These objects have meanings and symbolize your life and love. In identifying these, you are reminding yourselves of your deep love and connection. Keeping these symbols keeps the love alive.

SPENDING TIME

In order to keep the love alive, you must also be aware of how you are spending your time. Work, family and the fast-paced nature of modern life can be overwhelming and confusing and sometimes we forget to spend time on what is important. Spending quality time with your partner is great, but in order to create a long-lasting and solid relationship, spending time without your partner is just as important!

SPENDING TIME APART

Most successful marriages and relationships value the importance of the individuals in the couple. The idea that love means that you are each other's other half and you cannot be whole without one another is ultimately damaging when pursuing a long-lasting and healthy relationship. When you are with someone for a long time there is a risk of losing or forgetting who you are as a person. This can create resentment and conflict in the relationship, so it is important to take time for yourself outside your relationship.

Identify your hobbies and friends. Ask yourself if you have any that you do not share with your partner. If not, perhaps try to find things that you can do without your partner to remind yourself of your individuality. Taking up an evening class is a great way of doing this. Have you ever fancied learning to knit? Or singing in a choir? All these community events and classes are great ways to help you and your partner feel comfortable in your individuality.

Most of the time, spending time apart actually brings you and your partner together! There is something lovely about spending a day doing your own thing and then coming home and reconnecting with your partner, telling them about what you have learnt or done that day. If you have taken up hiking, remember to take some pictures to show your partner! Similarly, if you enroll in a pottery class, bringing home something you have made for your partner is a romantic and beautiful gesture.

SPENDING TIME TOGETHER

Taking up hobbies and friends outside your relationship also means that when you spend time together, you truly appreciate one another. Take up hobbies apart, but also take up hobbies together! Trying new things as a team can be a great way to put that magic back into your relationship and remind you of why you fell in love in the first place. Ultimately, relationships are about having fun together as a pair and enjoying all the wonderful things that life can offer!

Figure 11

Have you ever been to the theatre together? Have you ever swam in the sea together? The world provides us with countless options and new experiences to bond you and your partner together. If Sunday comes around and you both are free, be spontaneous! Find magic in nature, walking or picnicking in a park or a forest. Every month, try to do one thing that at least one of you has not done before.

Spending quality time together is worth more than anything else in a relationship. Enjoying life and supporting one another is the end goal for your partnership and should not be forgotten. Be grateful for one another, you picked each other for a reason. Sometimes we forget these reasons and forget to be grateful. Remind yourself every morning of why you are with your partner and every time they remind you of why you love them, hold onto this. Treasure this feeling of love and support, and know that you can work through whatever life throws at you.

Hopefully, this book has given you reasons to believe in long-lasting love. It is possible for love and romance to last a lifetime; all it takes are the right tools to help you out. No relationship is the same and there is no one-size-fits-all formula for the perfect relationship, but this book can be used as a general guide to build on your love for one another.

Putting in work to make that honeymoon phase last forever can be done with the right attitude and with the right partner. Nobody is perfect, not even the person you fall in love with, but in your eyes they can be nearly perfect! This is good enough!

Conflict and arguments are inevitable, it would be weird if they did not occur in a relationship. But now, because of this book, you are able to recognize different types of conflict and healthy and unhealthy ways of approaching them. The key is always communicating in a respectful and constructive manner and this book has guided you through that. Finding your way through conflict will be so rewarding as it will give you and your partner a concrete and solid partnership, allowing you to retain your individuality but also recognize the beauty and gifts that being in a relationship gives you.

Remember the metaphor of the brick wall? How building a relationship is like building a wall and every single brick matters in supporting the others? Look at your relationship and examine the bricks. Make sure none has any cracks. Is the brick wall a house and a home yet? Perhaps there is still work to do, but when that wall becomes a home you will thank yourself for putting in the work together. Remember to check for cracks regularly, and do this by open and honest communication.

For single people, hopefully, this book has given you excitement and encouragement to date and find love! Having these tools ready means that you are well-equipped to take on any troubles a relationship may have. The book has provided you with ways and information about how to build a healthy and happy relationship.

At its core, a relationship should allow and support both parties to enjoy and experience life. Life, love and sex are the most beautiful things, and everybody should have the opportunity of experiencing them!

REFERENCES

Centers for Disease Control and Prevention. HIV Surveillance Report, 2018 (Updated); vol. 31.http://www.cdc.gov/hiv/library/reports/hiv-surveillance.html.

Chapman, G. D. (2004). *The 5 Love Languages: The Secret To Love That Lasts*. Chicago: Northfield Publishing.

Durex. The Orgasm Gap. (n.d.). Retrieved August 8, 2020, from https://www.durex.co.uk/blogs/explore-sex/the-orgasm-gap

Figure 1: Man Kissing Woman on Check Beside Body of Water, by Esther Ann, 2017. https://unsplash.com/photos/glpYh1cWf0o

Figure 2: Woman Wearing While Cardigan. From Unsplash, by Priscilla Du Preez, 2016. https://unsplash.com/photos/_TGDr3nPLSY

Figure 3: Man and Woman Holding a Heart Together. From Unsplash, by Kelly Sikkema, 2020. https://unsplash.com/photos/4le7k9XVYjE

Figure 4: Man and Woman Breakfast in bed. From Unsplash, by Toa Heftiba. 2017/ https://unsplash.com/photos/60bpHzzh_yc/info

Figure 5: The Argument. From Unsplash, by Mike Lloyd, 2018. https://unsplash.com/photos/ksWKFRLi85I

Figure 6: Couple Issues. From Unsplash, by Damir Spanic, 2020. https://unsplash.com/photos/8SuZ4l4C3FA

Figure 7: Plus Size Women in Bed Reading Book and Phone With Dog. From Unsplash, by AllGo, 2019. https://unsplash.com/photos/1VAmHZktnso

Figure 8: Silhouette of Man and Woman about to Kiss, by frank Mckenna, 2017. https://unsplash.com/photos/A9kYGeJkMZE

Figure 9: Hearts. From Unsplash, by Jude Beck, 2020. https://unsplash.com/photos/m7kd1cRxu48

Figure 10: Man and Woman Smiling. From Unsplash, by Alesia Kazantceva, 2018. https://unsplash.com/photos/ESGJoEl8bcU

Figure 11: Don't Let Go. From Unsplash, by Everton Vila, 2016. https://unsplash.com/photos/AsahNlCoVhQ

Gottman, J. M., & Silver, N. (2015). *The Seven Principles For Making Marriage Work:* New York: Crown.

Kuriansky, J. (2002) *The Complete Idiots Guide to Tantric Sex:* Indianapolis: Alpha Books.

Waring, B. (2006) *NIH Record Vol. LVIII, No. 4: A Cuddle a Day Keeps The Doctor Away.* Maryland: Editorial Operations Branch, Office of Communications and Public Liaison.